CREATED
2
CREATE

CREATED 2 CREATE

UNLEASHING KINGDOM CREATIVITY THROUGH PRAYER

BY: DESIREE DANIELLE

Created 2 Create

© 2025 Desiree Danielle

Published by Desiree Danielle/ Birmingham, Al

ISBN: 979-8-218-81553-0

First Edition

Printed in the United States of America

TABLE OF CONTENTS

4. THE BATTLE FOR CREATIVITY

– Overcoming Resistance Through Intercession

When fear, comparison, and distraction try to silence your yes.

5. CREATING WITH PURPOSE

– Aligning With Kingdom Vision
Moving beyond performance into purpose.

6. SUSTAINING THE FLOW

– Making Prayer a Creative Lifestyle
Staying connected to the Source as you create.

7. RELEASE WHAT'S IN YOU

– Creating From Legacy
Boldly unleashing what God placed in your hands.

CONCLUSION

– A Final Charge
A call to release, steward, and carry legacy well.

AUTHOR'S NOTE

Before you dive into these pages, I want to share a little about who I am and why this book exists.

I'm a writer, a photographer, a podcast producer, a licensed cosmetologist, and a worship dancer —a creative who never really fits inside one box. For a long time, I thought I had to choose. I wondered if the way God wired me—to flow in multiple spaces, to see beauty in business and ministry, to build, design, pray, and create—was too much. Or maybe not enough.

But over time, the Holy Spirit began to show me that all of it was worship. That every space I walked into was sacred ground when I let Him lead. That which seemed scattered was actually strategic. That my creativity wasn't just about talent—it was about obedience.

I've heard God speak behind the camera, at the salon chair, and in the silence of a blank screen. I've felt His presence while editing someone else's voice and while searching for my own. I've walked through wilderness seasons where I buried what He gave me out of fear. And I've lived through moments of divine flow where His Spirit breathed on my yes.

I don't write this book as someone who has mastered it all. I write as someone who has been shaped by the process—formed like clay in the hands of the Potter. Still learning. Still yielding and still saying yes.

Created 2 Create was birthed through prayer, process, and the quiet moments where God reminded me that creativity is not just something we do—it's who we are. This is not a how-to manual. It's a conversation. A companion. A call to co-create with God, not for performance, but for purpose.

As you read, I encourage you to pause when something stirs you. Don't rush. Let it sit. Let God speak.

You'll find space throughout the book—blank pages between chapters—for your own reflections, prayers, or creative thoughts. Use them freely. This book is not just my voice—it's an invitation to hear God in your own.

We were created to create. And Heaven is still waiting on your yes.

With love,

Desiree Danielle

INTRODUCTION

CREATED 2 CREATE: UNLOCKING KINGDOM CREATIVITY THROUGH PRAYER

Let me start by saying this: if you're holding this book, it's not by accident. I don't know how it ended up in your hands—whether you stumbled on it while scrolling, someone gifted it to you, or you felt a gentle nudge to pick it up—but I genuinely believe you're here on purpose.

You might be an artist, a writer, a dancer, a musician, a photographer, a business owner, or a speaker. Maybe you're someone who has a lot of creative ideas that you've never had the time or space to explore. Or maybe you're carrying something so deep in your spirit that you don't even have words for it yet—but you know there's something in you. Something God-breathed. Something waiting to be released.

Here's what I know: we were created by the ultimate Creator. The very first thing we learn about God in Scripture is that He created.
"In the beginning, God created the heavens and the earth." (Genesis 1:1)
Before he healed. Before he delivered. Before He even spoke to Adam and Eve, He created. That's how He chose to introduce Himself to us, as a Creator.

And then, just a few verses later, He made us.
"Let us make human beings in our image, to be like us..." (Genesis 1:26)

That means creativity isn't reserved for the "artsy" folks. It's not just a personality trait or a natural talent. Creativity is part of our design. It's part of what it means to be made in God's image. Whether you create with words, with colors, with movement, with strategy, with vision, or with your hands—you were created to create.

But I know how life can make us forget that.
Some of us had our creativity criticized, downplayed, or ignored.
Some of us had to survive, so we set our creative dreams to the side.
Some of us tried to use our gifts, only to run into walls of fear, comparison, perfectionism, or burnout.
And for some, religion may have made you feel like your creative expression didn't "fit."

You're not alone in that.

But here's what I've come to know:
Creativity is not just something we do—it's one of the ways God moves through us. It's one of the ways He speaks. How He brings healing, beauty, truth, and transformation into the earth.

And when it's surrendered to Him, creativity becomes more than just a gift—it becomes an assignment.

That's where prayer comes in.

Prayer is the key that unlocks Kingdom creativity.
I'm not just talking about the quick "Lord help me" prayers we whisper when we're stuck (although those matter too). I'm talking about real prayer—consistent, intentional communion with the One who placed the gift inside of you to begin with.

Prayer is what grounds us when doubt creeps in.
Prayer is what breaks through the fog when we're dry

or uninspired.

Prayer is what breathes clarity into vision and strategy into execution.
Prayer is what shifts our creativity from being just for us to being for His glory.

This book is part testimony, part teaching, and all about partnership with the Holy Spirit.
You'll learn who He is, how He wants to walk with you through the creative process, and what it looks like to build something that carries Kingdom weight and eternal purpose.

Throughout the chapters, I'll share scriptures, reflections, and prayers—some vulnerable moments, some lessons I learned the hard way, and some that still surprise me. Each page is an invitation to pause, reflect, and lean in deeper.

Whether you're just beginning or you've been creating for years, I want this book to feel like a conversation. Like a safe space to remember who you are, why it matters, and how to flow with the One who placed something inside of you that is still waiting to be released.

I don't believe in pressure-based creativity. I believe in presence-led creativity.
The best ideas are the ones birthed in prayer.
I believe that when you create with God, you create from a place of rest—not striving.
And I believe that what's inside of you is needed now more than ever.

If you've been discouraged, distracted, or disconnected from the creative part of yourself, this is your invitation to reconnect with the One who gave

you the gift.
If you've been creating, but want to go deeper—this is your invitation to co-create with Him in a new way.
If you've buried your gift, this is your invitation to dig it back up.

It's not too late.
You're not too far behind.
And you don't have to do it in your own strength.

You were created to create. And it's time to unlock what's been waiting in you for far too long.

PRAYER

God,
Thank You for being the original Creator—the One who formed the heavens and the earth... and still takes time to form me.

You knit me together in my mother's womb. You saw every part of me before I ever created a thing. And today, I stand in awe—not just of who You are, but of how You made me. I praise You because I am fearfully and wonderfully made; Your works are wonderful. My soul knows that well. (Psalm 139:13–14)

You didn't just give me breath—You gave me purpose. You crafted me for something eternal. I am Your workmanship—created in Christ Jesus for good works that You prepared beforehand. (Ephesians 2:10)

And so I offer it all back to You. My body, my mind, my creativity—let it be a living sacrifice. Holy. Acceptable. Set apart for You. (Romans 12:1)

Shape me, Lord. You are the Potter, and I am the clay. (Isaiah 64:8)
Mold my heart. Refine my gift.
And even when You reshape what I thought I understood—help me to trust the hands that formed me.

Fill me like You filled Bezalel—with Your Spirit, with wisdom, with understanding, with knowledge, and with skill to create and build what's on Your heart. (Exodus 31:3–5)
Not for my glory. Not for performance. But for Your glory alone.

I don't want to create from striving—I want to create from surrender.
Let my creativity be worship. Let it carry Your presence.
Whatever I do, let me work at it with all my heart, as working for the Lord, not for man. For it is You, Christ, I ultimately serve. (Colossians 3:23–24)

Show me what to build. Show me how to release what You've placed in me.
Make Your ways known to me, Lord. Teach me Your

paths. Guide me in Your truth and teach me, for You are God my Savior, and my hope is in You all day long. (Psalm 25:4–5)

Holy Spirit, lead this journey.
Speak to the places in me that have been hidden,

silenced, or buried. Ignite every dormant thing.
And breathe on what You've entrusted me to carry.

In Jesus' name,
Amen.

CHAPTER 1:

THE CREATOR — THE ORIGINAL SOURCE OF CREATIVITY

"In the beginning, God created the heavens and the earth." (Genesis 1:1)

Before we go any further, we need to start at the beginning. Not just the beginning of this book — but the beginning of all things.

When you open scripture, the very first thing you learn about God isn't that He's powerful (though He is), or holy (which He absolutely is), or even loving (though that's His very nature). The first thing God shows us about Himself is this: He creates.

God, in all His glory, chose to begin His story with creativity. Not because He needed to, but because He wanted to. Before there was light. Before there were stars, sounds, or systems. Before humanity even took its first breath, there was a Creator at work.

That alone tells us something. It tells us that creativity is sacred. It's not a side note in God's story — it's the opening line. It's not extra. It's embedded in who He is. And if it's embedded in Him — and we are made in His image — then it's embedded in us too.

When I think about creativity, my mind doesn't just go to paintbrushes, songs, or photographs. I think about my mom. Growing up, there were plenty of days when our pantry looked scarce. Yet somehow, she would take a few simple ingredients and pull together a meal that not only filled our stomachs but became some of my favorite dishes to this day. At the time, I thought it was just "good cooking." Now I realize it was creativity. She was building with what she had, solving problems with love and resourcefulness.

That's the truth about creativity: it's not limited to a canvas or a stage. Creativity is in the way you parent, the way you solve problems, the way you organize chaos into order. It's in the way you stretch a meal, build a business, or navigate hard seasons with wisdom you didn't know you carried. All of that reflects Elohim — the Creator God whose image you bear.

So before we disqualify ourselves by saying "I'm not creative," we have to pause and ask: Am I reflecting my Father's nature? Am I building, shaping, or bringing forth something that wasn't there before? If the answer is yes, then you are walking in creativity.

A CREATOR IN MOTION

I don't know about you, but I can't read Genesis 1 without feeling like I'm watching a masterpiece unfold. The earth was formless, dark, and void. And then — movement.

"Now the earth was formless and empty, darkness was over the surface of the deep, and the Spirit of God was hovering over the waters." (Genesis 1:2)

The Spirit of God hovered like an artist preparing a canvas. He spoke, and light broke into darkness. He separated the waters and raised the sky like a dome. He sculpted the land, planted lush gardens, and filled the atmosphere with sound, color, and life.

And then He created us.

Not as an afterthought. Not as something separate from His creative process. But as part of it. "So God created mankind in his own image, in the image of God he created them; male and female he created them." (Genesis 1:27)

He made us in His image — His creative image. And then He handed us the baton and said, "Be fruitful. Multiply. Fill the earth. Govern it." (Genesis 1:28)

Translation? Now you create.

We weren't just created by creativity — we were created for creativity. And every time we build, nurture, solve, or bring something new into existence, we echo the Creator who breathed life into us.

WHEN CREATING FEELS LIKE WORSHIP

There are moments when creating feels like pure worship.

I've felt it behind the camera, watching light wrap around a subject like a hug from heaven. I've felt it editing footage late at night, sensing the Holy Spirit breathe through what I thought was just "content." But one moment I'll never forget happened right behind the chair.

I was shampooing a client — someone who usually talked the entire time. She's full of life and always has something to say. But that day, she lay back quietly. A small smile touched her face, but tears streamed down her cheeks.

I didn't ask questions. I just gave her the best shampoo I could and silently began to pray. I knew the Holy Spirit was already present.

Afterward, she looked at me and said, "I needed that so much." She and her husband were expecting their daughter, and recent tests had revealed a possible Down syndrome diagnosis. She told me, "As I was lying there, I just kept sensing God saying that everything was going to be alright."

That moment had nothing to do with the hairstyle. It had everything to do with the atmosphere. With presence. With peace. That's worship.

Because worship isn't just what we sing, it's what we offer. And when we offer our creativity back to God — even in the most ordinary, everyday tasks — we create space for Him to move.

WHEN CREATING FEELS LIKE WARFARE

But then there are other times.

Times when you sit with a blank page and the only thing louder than the silence is the voice of fear. Times when you've created something beautiful, but doubt creeps in and whispers, "It's not good enough." Times when comparison chokes your inspiration before you can even start.

I've been there more times than I'd like to admit.

There was a project I poured my heart into. I stayed up editing, praying, giving my all. When I finally shared it, the response was… silence. No comments. No engagement. And the voice of insecurity got loud: "Maybe that wasn't God. Maybe this isn't working. Maybe you're just doing too much."

But even in that silence, I felt God whisper, "Your obedience still counts."

See, we tend to only measure creativity by how it's received. But God measures it by how it's released.

Both worship and warfare can be holy. Both require obedience.
Some creations will come through communion. Others will be birthed through resistance.
But both are sacred when you offer them to God

CREATIVITY THAT WAS NEVER MEANT TO STOP

Creativity was never meant to stop because it was never just about us. From the beginning, God designed us as vessels of His Spirit — carriers of His presence. That means everything we create carries more weight than we realize.

"Do you not know that your bodies are temples of the Holy Spirit, who is in you, whom you have received from God? You are not your own; you were bought at a price. Therefore, honor God with your bodies." (1 Corinthians 6:19–20)

When Paul reminds us of this truth, it's not just about physical purity — it's about identity. If your body is a temple, then your creativity is worship. Every idea, every solution, every act of building, parenting, cooking, leading, or designing becomes a way to honor the God who dwells in you.

This changes everything. It means creativity doesn't start and end with our skillset — it flows from the Spirit of God within us. And if His Spirit is in you, then your creativity was never meant to be silenced, buried, or minimized. It was bought at a price, and it carries His presence into the world.

WHAT THE CHURCH AND CULTURE GOT WRONG

If creativity is divine, how have we allowed the world — or even the Church — to strip it of its value?

Culture has commercialized it. The Church has compartmentalized it.

I've seen creatives burn out chasing trends just to stay relevant. I've also seen people who feel deeply creative but never feel seen in church unless they're on stage or part of a production team. And for a long time, I wrestled with that myself.

I was building, styling, filming, editing, ministering —
and I didn't know if it was "enough" because it didn't
look like traditional ministry. But then God reminded
me: creativity is a form of ministry. When it's done with
Him, it carries His glory.

That's what both culture and church have missed.
Creativity was never meant to be confined to
performance or profit. It was always meant to carry
His presence. To shift atmospheres. To intercede. To
release Heaven on earth.

YOUR EXPRESSION MATTERS

Let me say this clearly:
Your creativity doesn't have to look like anyone else's.

Look around creation. God doesn't repeat Himself.
No two sunsets are the same.
No two fingerprints.
No two voices, rhythms, or smiles.

God's creativity is wildly diverse — and so is yours.
That means your unique expression is not only
welcome, it's necessary.

When you honor your creative voice, you reflect a
part of God that the world might not see in any other
way. And when you withhold it, that reflection remains
hidden.

YOU ARE NOT CREATING BY ACCIDENT

If you're reading this and there's a fire in you to write, sing, photograph, design, dance, teach, build, nurture, organize, or speak life into others — please hear this:

That is not random.
That is not small.
That is not extra.

That's Heaven's imprint.

God placed something inside you that this generation needs. And it doesn't have to be flashy. It doesn't have to fit the algorithm. It just needs to be faithful.

You were made in the image of the Creator — on purpose, with purpose. And someone needs what you carry, even if it's not for the masses, even if it's for one.

And when you create in obedience — whether for the one or the many — it still matters to God.

REFLECT

Let's pause here for a moment.

- Where have you buried your creativity or minimized its value?

- Have you been waiting for permission to embrace what God already placed in you?

- Do you still believe your creativity is sacred?

- What would change if you saw your gift as a reflection of God's image, not just a skill to develop?

LET'S PRAY

God, thank You for being the first Creator — the origin of beauty, the source of all inspiration. Thank You for shaping me in Your image, not just to exist but to create alongside You.

Teach me how to honor You with the work of my hands. Let my creativity flow from a heart fully yielded to You. I don't want to create for attention or applause; I want to create with intention, knowing that when I give You my best, I am working unto You (Colossians 3:23).

Remind me that I am not serving people — I am serving You. You see every offering, every unseen moment, every quiet yes. And You promise to reward faithfulness, even when no one else notices (Colossians 3:24).

Help me create with my whole heart. To reflect You well. To remember that when I create with You, it becomes worship.

So I give You every idea, every gift, every ounce of courage I have. Breathe on it. Use it. Let it bring You glory.

In Jesus' name, Amen.

CHAPTER 2:

WHO IS THE HOLY SPIRIT? — YOUR CREATIVE PARTNER

"But when the Father sends the Advocate as my representative — that is, the Holy Spirit — He will teach you everything and will remind you of everything I have told you."
— John 14:26 (NLT)

Before I began inviting the Holy Spirit into my creative work, I carried a great deal of pressure. I thought it was all on me — to be original, to be perfect, to be impressive. I'd pray about my work, but I wasn't truly creating with God. It felt more like asking Him to bless what I had already decided to do.

And if I'm honest, that pressure almost crushed me.

One day, there was a shift. Not in a thunderous way, but quietly. I was working on a project I had prayed for, one I thought would fulfill me, but now that I had it, I felt like I was drowning. I sat down, exhausted, and whispered, "Lord, I can't do this." It wasn't a complaint — it was a release. And in that moment, I sensed Him so clearly:

"You were never supposed to do it alone."

FROM PERFORMANCE TO PARTNERSHIP

The difference between creating for God and creating with Him is everything.

Creating for God feels like a performance. You constantly wonder: Is this good enough? Does this honor Him? Am I missing it?
But creating with God feels like a partnership. There's flow. There's freedom. There's room to mess up, pause, start again — and not feel like you've failed.

When you create for God, you feel pressure.
When you create with God, you feel peace.

That's the beauty of the Holy Spirit. He's not just the Comforter when you're going through something. He's the Creative Director when you're building something. He doesn't just point to your purpose — He walks with you in it. He reminds you. He teaches you. He even breathes on what you've already started.

The Holy Spirit is not distant. He is personal. Intimate. Present.
He's in the edits. The script. The sketch. The silence. And he has never once been unoriginal.

HE'S BEEN HOVERING SINCE THE BEGINNING

Before there was anything — before light, before form, before beauty — there was chaos. And He was there.

"Now the earth was formless and empty, darkness was over the surface of the deep, and the Spirit of God was hovering over the waters." (Genesis 1:2, NIV)

That word hovering is powerful. In Hebrew, it's rachaph — like a mother bird brooding gently over her young, protective and purposeful. It's not passive. It's intentional. Holy Spirit wasn't avoiding the chaos — He was hovering over it, ready to partner with what God would speak next.

Even in the dark. Even when things were wild and out

of control.

He was there. Preparing. Watching. Waiting.

It's the same in our lives. The places that feel formless, the spaces that feel empty — that's where He's most present. He moves in the deep, unseen places. He hovers over the parts of us we think are too messy or unworthy. And when the Word goes forth? Creation begins.

This isn't just a Genesis story. It's your story too

VESSELS CARRY PRESENCE, NOT PRESSURE

This is where so many of us get stuck. We've been trained to be producers.

Producers know how to get things done. They have deadlines, deliverables, and desired outcomes. They measure progress in output. They feel accomplished when something is finished, posted, launched, or shared. And honestly? There's nothing wrong with producing — the world rewards it.

But in the Kingdom, God isn't looking for producers. He's looking for vessels.

A producer needs control.
A vessel yields.

A producer asks, "What's next on the list?"

A vessel asks, "Holy Spirit, what are You saying?"

A producer moves by pressure — the pressure to stay relevant, to prove they're good enough, to meet expectations.
But a vessel moves by presence — sensitive to the Spirit, open to pause, willing to scrap the plan if it means staying aligned.

And here's the truth: "Not by might, nor by power, but by my Spirit," says the Lord Almighty. (Zechariah 4:6)

Shifting from producer to vessel doesn't happen overnight, especially for those of us raised in systems that praised performance more than presence. We were celebrated for being "on it," for producing under pressure, for making things happen.

But here's the truth:
You can produce for God and miss Him entirely.

I've done it.

I've also learned to adapt and shift.

I used to just do hair and make money. That was the goal — stay booked and busy. However, over time, the Lord began to reveal something deeper to me. This wasn't just about hair — it was about atmosphere, about assignment. He was allowing me to create a safe space where women could encounter His presence.

That shift didn't come with lightning. It came with stewardship.

The Holy Spirit began showing me how to budget my

time and money differently. I scheduled more margin between clients so I wasn't rushing from one person to the next. And something happened in that space. It got quiet — not every appointment was filled with conversation. Sometimes it was just the sound of worship music playing while she sat in stillness.

But even in that silence, I knew God was moving.

I didn't have to force the moment. I didn't have to perform.
I was simply a vessel.

And I became confident — not just in the style I gave her, but in the peace she left with. She walked away with her beauty restored, her spirit lifted, her soul reminded of God's love. Sometimes through words, sometimes through stillness, but always through presence.

WHEN CREATIVITY BECAME COMMUNION

That's what happens when you stop performing and start partnering. The shift isn't just external — it's deeply internal.

My prayers changed. Instead of "God help me get this done," it became, "Holy Spirit, what do You want to do here?"

I started to invite Him into every part of the process —
Behind the chair.
Behind the camera.
Behind the scenes.
Behind the overwhelm.

And it became communion.

REFLECTION QUESTIONS

Let these settle in your spirit:

- Have you been creating alone?

- Where are you carrying pressure instead of presence?

- What would shift if you trusted the Spirit to lead instead of proving you can do it on your own?

Create some time this week and invite Holy Spirit to hover with you. Let Him brood over the chaos, the unfinished, and the unseen. Ask him what He's preparing to speak.

LET'S PRAY

Holy Spirit, I welcome You into this creative space — not as an afterthought, but as my Partner. I repent for the times I've tried to carry the weight on my own.

Teach me to create with You.

Remind me that it is not by might, nor by power, but by Your Spirit (Zechariah 4:6). Remind me that You are the One who teaches me and brings to remembrance all that Jesus has said (John 14:26).

Show me what it looks like to flow with You — not rushing ahead, not falling behind, but moving in step with Your Spirit. Make me a vessel, not a performer. Not a producer. Just a vessel that carries Your presence.

Breathe on my ideas, my gifts, and my hands. Let my creativity be communion with You, and let it bring glory back to the Father.

In Jesus' name, Amen.

CHAPTER 3:

PARTNERING WITH THE HOLY SPIRIT IN THE CREATIVE PROCESS

"I have filled him with the Spirit of God… to make artistic designs…" (Exodus 31:2–4)

There's a difference between creating from inspiration and creating from intimacy. Inspiration is fleeting. Intimacy sustains. And when it's Spirit-led? It multiplies.

The men who built the tabernacle in Exodus weren't just skilled — they were Spirit-filled. That's what made their designs holy. And that same Spirit still fills us today.

I used to think creativity was about having the right conditions — a quiet space, good lighting, the perfect playlist. But what happens when the environment isn't ideal? What happens when the ideas stall or when everything feels off? What happens when your plans get interrupted — and the Holy Spirit shows up with something better?

The Holy Spirit is not a last-minute consultant. He's the Creative Director. He doesn't just inspire the vision — He guides the execution.

CREATIVITY AS OBEDIENCE

What if the creative process wasn't about getting it "right," but about getting in rhythm with God?

What if, instead of asking, "Is this good enough?" we asked, "Is this what God asked me to do?"

Sometimes we're so focused on the final product that we forget the most powerful thing we bring into any space is our yes.

Not our perfection.
Not our performance.
Just our posture.

That kind of posture shifts everything. Because obedience doesn't always look productive, sometimes it looks like waiting. Like deleting everything and starting over. Like releasing something before you feel "ready."

Obedience is the fruit of intimacy.

WHEN GOD RESHAPES THE PLAN

There's a passage in Jeremiah that always humbles me — and honestly, it reads a lot like my creative process:

"So I went down to the potter's house, and I saw him working at the wheel. But the pot he was shaping from the clay was marred in his hands; so the potter formed it into another pot, shaping it as seemed best to him." (Jeremiah 18:3–4, NIV)

That line hits different when you're a creative. Because there are times you know God gave you something — a vision, a design, a story — and then He suddenly reshapes it. Not because you failed. Not because it wasn't good. But simply because He's the Potter, and you're the clay.

That's precisely what happened to me during a shoot for Women of Hope magazine.

I had everything planned — the studio was booked, the vision was solid, and I had just finished doing the client's makeup. Ten minutes before we were supposed to leave for the studio, I got a message that changed everything: the studio was no longer available due to some unforeseen circumstances.

Now, I wish I could say I immediately responded with faith, but for a second, all the worst-case thoughts rushed in: What am I supposed to do now? What if this whole thing flops?

But instead of panicking, I took a breath and remembered a library I'd shot at before. As we headed that way, I started mapping out the inside in my head. But as we walked in, I glanced to my right and saw a covered walkway outside. Nothing fancy. I had passed it before and never paid it any attention. But this time, it felt like a nudge—a redirection.

We didn't shoot inside that day. We didn't follow my plan.

We shot right there, under that walkway. And when I tell you those images turned out so good? I mean it. Not just "make it work" good, but God breathed on it good.

That moment reminded me: I'm not just the photographer. I'm not just the visionary. I'm the clay. And when the Holy Spirit says, "Let Me reshape this," the only proper response is, "Yes, Lord."

Romans 9:21 says, "Does not the potter have the right to make out of the same lump of clay some pottery for special purposes and some for common use?"

It's not always about the plan — it's about the Potter. It's not about controlling the outcome — it's about trusting the hands you're in.

I thought I was shooting a cover.
God was reminding me to surrender.

FROM PRODUCING TO LISTENING

There's a constant temptation to measure creativity by output:
How much did you create this month? Did it get engagement? Did it sell?

However, the Kingdom doesn't measure fruitfulness in the same way the world does.

The world rewards hustle.
Heaven honors surrender.

We're not called to hustle for God — we're called to move with Him.

That means you might walk through seasons of fire and flow, followed by seasons of pause and pruning.
Both are holy.
Both require trust.

LETTING GO OF PERFECT

There's a lie that says if it's not polished, it's not powerful. But some of the most anointed things I've ever created were raw. Imperfect. Honest.

Sometimes God will ask you to release it before you refine it.
Sometimes he'll whisper, "You're done. Let it go."

Even when you still want to tweak the caption, re-edit the clip, or overthink the post.

There's freedom in that. Because God doesn't anoint perfection, he anoints obedience.

REFLECTION QUESTIONS

Where are you resisting the reshaping?

- What are you clinging to that God may be asking you to release?

- Are you willing to let the Holy Spirit change the location, the angle, or even the entire vision?

- What would it look like to commit your creative process fully to Him, trusting He will establish the plans? (Proverbs 16:3)

LET'S PRAY

Holy Spirit, I invite you into every part of my creative process — not just the outcome, but the in-between moments. The messy drafts. The pauses. The redirections.

Help me trust You more than I trust my plans. Teach me to listen, to yield, and to create in rhythm with You. I don't want just to make things; I want to move with You.

Remind me that if You are in it, it is already enough. And as Proverbs 16:3 says, I commit my work to You, trusting that You will establish my plans.

I choose obedience over perfection, surrender over striving. Shape me as You see best, Potter, and let my yes echo Your glory.

In Jesus' name, Amen.

CHAPTER 4:

THE BATTLE FOR CREATIVITY — OVER-COMING RESISTANCE THROUGH INTERCESSION

"For we wrestle not against flesh and blood, but against principalities, against powers, against the rulers of the darkness of this world…" (Ephesians 6:12)

Let's talk about what most creatives don't say out loud. The moments when your heart feels full of vision, but your hands won't move. Every time you try to create, something comes to steal your focus, your energy, your confidence.

There is real resistance in the creative space. And it's not always coming from outside of you. Sometimes warfare shows up in your thoughts, your patterns, and your fear of being misunderstood. And sometimes, it's deeply spiritual.

CREATIVITY COMES WITH A TARGET

If you've ever sat down to write, paint, plan, or record — only to be hit with a wave of insecurity or distraction — then you've encountered it. The battle. That invisible pressure that tells you, This doesn't matter. No one will care. You're not good enough.

Sound familiar?

Paul reminds us in Ephesians that we don't wrestle against flesh and blood. So, when we experience tension in our creativity, we must discern: Is this just a bad day, or is this spiritual warfare trying to shut me down?

The enemy doesn't waste time on what doesn't matter. He targets what carries weight. And if your creativity reflects Heaven — if your words, your visuals, your work make room for God's presence — then it's not just art. It's a weapon.

And weapons draw fire.

RESISTANCE HAS A NAME

Over the years, I've come to recognize resistance more clearly. It wears different faces:

- **Perfectionism** — the voice that says, "Don't release it until it's flawless."

- **Comparison** — "She already did it better."

- **Distraction** — endless scrolling, fatigue, or busyness that steals your margin.

- **Fear** — fear of being seen, fear of not being seen, fear of failure, fear of success.

Some of these voices even sound like our own. But they're rooted in lies, subtle enough to feel logical: Be careful. Take your time. Wait until it's perfect.

But Holy Spirit never leads with anxiety. He always invites with peace — even when it isn't easy.

The first step to overcoming resistance is to name it. Expose it. Call it what it is.

THE FEAR OF BEING SEEN
VS.
NOT BEING SEEN

This one runs deep.

Some of us hide our creativity because we're afraid of what people will think if we share it. We don't want to be misunderstood. We don't want to be judged.

Others pour their heart into something, release it, and hear… silence. No response. No affirmation. And it feels like invisibility.

Both fears are real. Both can stop us from creating altogether. But here's the truth: God sees it all. Whether one listens or a thousand, whether people clap or scroll by — He sees you. He honors obedience over outcome. And Heaven keeps score differently.

WHEN INTERCESSION BROKE THE FOG

I remember working on a project that felt like walking through molasses. Every idea seemed stale. Every step is heavy. I kept second-guessing myself.

Finally, I stopped forcing it. I turned everything off and whispered, "Holy Spirit, I feel blocked. I don't know what this is, but I need you to clear it out."

No fancy words. Just hunger.

I prayed in the Spirit. I worshiped a little. Cried a little. Sat in silence. And slowly, the fog began to lift. It wasn't magic — it was presence.

That moment reminded me: this is not just creative work. It's spiritual work. Sometimes resistance isn't broken by more effort. It's broken by intercession.

YOUR CREATIVE RESISTANCE TOOLKIT

Sometimes what you're facing isn't just procrastination — it's spiritual. And when that's the case, you need more than motivation. You need tools that carry weight in the Spirit.

This toolkit isn't just a list. It's a practice—something to return to, pray through, and build into your rhythm.

1. DECLARATIONS: SPEAK TRUTH OVER THE LIES

Resistance often begins in the mind. Lies whisper things like: "You're not ready. You're not enough. No one cares."

That's why declarations matter. When you open your mouth and speak God's Word, you confront the lie with truth. Declarations shift the atmosphere — not because of your volume, but because of His authority.

Try these:

- "I create from a place of peace, not pressure." (Philippians 4:6–7)

- "My gift is needed in the earth." (1 Peter 4:10)

- "I release obedience, not perfection." (Matthew 11:28–30)

- "The Spirit who raised Jesus from the dead lives in me." (Romans 8:11)

- "I create with boldness, knowing Heaven backs me." (Acts 4:29–31)

Declarations remind your heart of what Heaven already knows: you are called, equipped, and covered.

2. PRAYERS: INVITE GOD INTO THE BATTLE

Sometimes resistance won't break by sheer effort. It breaks when you invite God into it.

Prayer is your lifeline. It silences lies, restores clarity, and fills you with strength that doesn't come from you. This is where 2 Corinthians 10:5 comes alive: "We take captive every thought to make it obedient to Christ."

Here's a prayer for the fog:

Holy Spirit, silence every voice that is not Yours. I take every thought captive and make it obedient to Christ (2 Corinthians 10:5). I come out of agreement with fear, shame, and perfectionism. Remind me who I am. Let Your truth override every lie. Give me grace to show up in faith, even in the tension. I trust You with the process. In Jesus' name, Amen.

This isn't about fancy words. It's about alignment. Every prayer invites the power of God into the middle of your process.

3. SCRIPTURE: LET THE WORD DO THE WORK

Feelings may shift, but God's Word never does. Scripture is sharper than any two-edged sword (Hebrews 4:12). When you read it, speak it, or tape it near your workspace, you anchor yourself to unshakable truth.

Keep these close when resistance rises:

- "The weapons of our warfare are not carnal, but mighty through God to the pulling down of strongholds." (2 Corinthians 10:4)

- "He who began a good work in you will carry it on to completion until the day of Christ Jesus." (Philippians 1:6)

- "For God has not given us a spirit of fear, but of power, love, and a sound mind." (2 Timothy 1:7)

When resistance rises, don't just scroll for inspiration. Let Scripture fight for you.

4. WORSHIP: SHIFT THE ATMOSPHERE

Sometimes resistance isn't in your head — it's in the atmosphere. The heaviness, the distraction, the fog. Worship breaks it.

- You don't need a stage or a set list. Sometimes it's one song, one lifted hand, or one whispered "Jesus" that changes everything.

- Worship reminds you of who God is, not just what you're facing.

- Worship re-centers your spirit on His presence, not your pressure.

- Worship invites breakthrough when words run dry.

Practical tip: Keep a short worship playlist ready for moments of resistance. Let worship become your weapon of choice when the room feels heavy.

5. STILLNESS: GUARD THE QUIET

If worship clears the air, stillness clears the heart.

Resistance thrives in noise — the constant scrolling, comparing, and overthinking that drowns out God's whisper. Stillness makes room for Him to speak.

- Stillness silences lies and creates space for truth.

- Stillness teaches you to wait instead of rushing.

- Stillness restores clarity when your mind feels cluttered.

Practical tip: Take five minutes of stillness each day. Phone down. Eyes closed. Heart open. Let the quiet reset your spirit and invite God's peace into the creative process.

REFLECTION QUESTIONS

- What voice are you listening to while you create?

- Are you shrinking out of fear or rising in your God-given identity?

- What resistance do you need to name today?

- Have you invited God into this process, or have

you been trying to push through alone?

LET'S PRAY

Father, thank You that we are not creating alone. You've equipped us with power, truth, and access to Your presence. When resistance rises, help us not to retreat but to press in. Teach us how to war well — with prayer, with truth, and with bold faith.

Let our creativity flow not just from talent, but from communion with You. We reject every lie that says we are not enough. We come into agreement with Your voice — the One who called us, gifted us, and still covers us today.

And we hold onto this truth: "If God is for us, who can be against us?" (Romans 8:31).

In Jesus' name, Amen.

CHAPTER 5:

CREATING WITH PURPOSE — OBEDIENCE IS THE NEW SUCCESS

"Whatever you do, work at it with all your heart, as working for the Lord, not for human masters, since you know that you will receive an inheritance from the Lord as a reward. It is the Lord Christ you are serving." (Colossians 3:23–24)

There's a moment in every creative journey when God whispers, "Is this still about Me?"

That question doesn't always come in a loud or dramatic way. Sometimes it sneaks in while you're editing a post or planning a launch. It rises when you're scrolling through highlight reels, feeling the pressure to keep up. It comes when your strategy stops flowing and your creativity feels dry. That question? It stops you in your tracks.

And it changes everything.

WHEN YOUR WHY GROWS UP

In the beginning, creating might feel light. Free. Expressive. But if you're truly following Jesus, there comes a shift—a holy disruption.

That's when the Lord starts dealing with your motives. He begins to uncover the hidden need to be validated, the unspoken hope that your work will be applauded. And He doesn't expose it to shame you — He brings it up to purify you. He wants your "yes" to be rooted in purpose, not pressure.

For me, it started behind the chair.

I have always loved doing hair. But I didn't always understand that it was a ministry. That it was a space God wanted to inhabit with me. The Holy Spirit taught me to slow down — not to squeeze in more clients, but to create space for His presence.

Sometimes that looked like silence. Just worship music playing softly while the weight of His presence rested in the room. And when clients left, it wasn't just with a new style. They left with peace. With strength. With something they didn't know they needed.

That's when my why grew up.

YOU'RE NOT JUST GIFTED — YOU'RE ENTRUSTED

When you realize your creativity is tied to someone else's breakthrough, you stop treating it casually. You stop winging it. You stop acting like it's optional.

You start to carry it differently. Not with pressure, but with purpose. With reverence. With the understanding that what God put in you wasn't just for you.

You weren't just called to express — you were called to impact.

EXCELLENCE IS WORSHIP, NOT PERFECTION

There's a lie that says everything has to be flawless: perfect photos, perfect lighting, perfect timing.

For a long time, I thought striving for perfection was

the same as pursuing excellence. But the Holy Spirit corrected me.

Perfection is about control.
 Excellence is about surrender.

Perfection asks, "What will people think of this?"
 Excellence asks, "How can I honor God with this?"

Excellence doesn't mean overthinking or constant tweaking. It means, "I did this with intention. I gave it my heart." That's worship. That's faithfulness. And that's enough.

CREATING FROM BURDEN, NOT BRANDING

Not everything God calls you to create will fit your brand.

Sometimes, He'll give you a word or idea that doesn't match your content plan. But it burns in your spirit. It won't let you go.

That's a burden.

Burden says, "This isn't about numbers. This is about obedience."

I once shared a raw, personal message. No fancy background. No curated caption. It didn't perform well. But the few who responded were deeply touched.

They needed that exact word in that exact moment.

That's the kind of fruit you can't track with metrics.

OBEDIENCE OVER ALGORITHMS

This is where it gets real, especially in the world of content creation.

The pressure to show up online is intense. There's a formula for everything: post three times a day, use trending sounds, stay consistent, and engage constantly.

And none of that is bad. There's wisdom in strategy. But here's the wrestle: what happens when the Holy Spirit leads you differently?

What if He tells you to pause, to post less, to release something "off-brand"? What if you pour your heart into a video and it only gets two views?

Are those two views as valuable as the 500 you were hoping for?

Would you still feel faithful? Or would you feel like you missed?

The temptation is to create for visibility. But the calling is to create out of obedience.

And obedience doesn't always get engagement. Sometimes it's quiet. Sometimes it's misunderstood. Sometimes it doesn't go viral — but it breaks something in the spirit. That's Kingdom.

KINGDOM METRICS HIT DIFFERENT

The world celebrates fruit that's visible.
 The Kingdom celebrates fruit that's eternal.

The world tells you to post more.
 The Spirit might tell you to pray more.

The world says, "Build your audience."
 The Kingdom says, "Tend your assignment."

We have to stop measuring our purpose by applause. God may call you to build something only a handful of people will see — but those few might be the very ones He's after.

Would you still say yes?

ANCHOR TRUTH

You are not behind.
You are not doing it wrong.
You are building differently — because you're building by the Spirit.

REFLECTION QUESTIONS

- What "normal business practices" am I clinging to that God may be asking me to release?

- Where is the Holy Spirit inviting me to create from a different rhythm?

- Am I willing to be obedient even if it doesn't look successful?

- Have I given God my algorithm or just my art?

- What would shift if I believed my gift was a Kingdom assignment, not just a talent?

LET'S PRAY

Father, I surrender my why. I surrender my rhythm. I surrender my desire to be seen. Forgive me for measuring success by the world's standards instead of Yours. Purify my motives. Teach me to create from obedience, not pressure. From burden, not branding.

Let my creativity serve Your Kingdom, not my ego. I don't want to build platforms — I want to build altars. Let everything I make point back to You, even when the numbers are low, even when the reach is small.

May faithfulness be my measure, and Your presence be my reward. And as Your Word says, "So whether you eat or drink or whatever you do, do it all for the glory of God." (1 Corinthians 10:31)

In Jesus' name, Amen.

CHAPTER 6:

SUSTAINING THE FLOW — MAKING PRAYER A CREATIVE LIFESTYLE

"Pray without ceasing." (1 Thessalonians 5:17)

I used to think prayer had to look a certain way. Worship music playing. Bible open. Journal nearby. House still.

And while those moments are beautiful and necessary, they're not always my reality.

Some days, I'm praying while holding a curling iron, asking the Holy Spirit to give me discernment for the woman in my chair. Other days, I'm editing a video and whispering, "Okay Lord… what's the story here?" More times than I can count, I've prayed in the car, in the store, or in the middle of a shoot.

That's prayer, too.

We seek flow in our creativity — those moments when everything feels aligned and ideas are pouring out. But if we want to sustain that flow, we must stay connected to the Source. Inspiration may spark something for a moment, but prayer sustains you for the journey.

Prayer doesn't always look polished. It's not always quiet or uninterrupted. But it is intentional. It is real.

PRAYER AS RHYTHM, NOT RITUAL

When Paul said "pray without ceasing," he wasn't commanding us to live in a prayer closet all day. He was inviting us to bring God into every part of life.

Not just the spiritual moments — all of it.

The drive to the studio.
 The conversation with your team.
 The moment you're staring at a blank canvas,
wondering what to make of it.

Prayer becomes rhythm. A constant awareness of
God's presence is woven into the fabric of life.

It's the pause before the pitch.
The whisper before the words.
The stillness in the middle of the scroll.

SPIRITUAL HYDRATION OVER HUSTLE CULTURE

Burnout doesn't always shout. Sometimes it's subtle:
numbness, a block you can't shake, the moment you
realize you've been producing but not abiding.

In a culture that glorifies hustle, it's easy to confuse
output with obedience. But fruit doesn't come from
striving. Fruit comes from staying.

Jesus said, "I am the vine; you are the branches. If
you remain in me and I in you, you will bear much
fruit; apart from me you can do nothing." (John 15:5)

Without spiritual hydration, even the most talented
creative will eventually run dry. You were never
designed to do this apart from Him.

MAKING ROOM FOR GOD ON PURPOSE

Let's talk about intentionality.

We plan our content.
We show up for clients.
We set alarms, attend meetings, and run errands like clockwork.

But do we meet with God with the same consistency?

If I'm honest, there were seasons when I prayed, but I didn't prioritize. I asked Him to bless what I'd already decided, instead of waiting to hear what He wanted to do.

The shift came when I moved from fitting Him in to centering everything around Him. It didn't require hours of stillness — it required surrender.

Now, I try to meet with God before I meet with the world. Before I open my planner. Before I step into creative work. Not perfectly — but intentionally.

And that one shift? It keeps my heart postured in the right direction.

CREATING FROM OVERFLOW, NOT EMPTINESS

What flows out of you creatively is always connected

to what's happening spiritually.

When I create without prayer, I feel it. I get distracted. I overthink. I compare. I start looking for approval instead of looking for God.

But when prayer becomes my foundation, even my flaws don't fluster me. There's clarity. There's peace. There's grace — even when the task feels heavy.

PRACTICAL WAYS TO BE INTENTIONAL WITH PRAYER

This doesn't have to be complicated. Let it be honest. Let it be sustainable.

- Start your day with God. Before your feet hit the ground or your phone lights up, offer Him your day. A simple "Here I am, Lord" is enough.

- Create Selah moments. Pause between tasks. Breathe. Ask Him, "What are you saying here?"

- Establish sacred space and rhythm. A prayer journal, a corner in your home, or worship before you open your laptop — whatever signals your spirit to invite Him in.

- Ask before you act. Before every shoot, session, or meeting, pause for 30 seconds: "Holy Spirit, lead me. Not my will — Yours."

- End your day in reflection. Thank Him. Repent if needed. Ask Him to cover your rest.

REFLECTION QUESTIONS

- Have I been creating from overflow or exhaustion?

- What would shift if I truly made God the priority?

- Where is the Holy Spirit inviting me to pause and realign with Him?

- Am I abiding, or just producing?

LET'S PRAY

Father, thank You for the gift of communion. Teach me to make prayer more than a moment — make it my way of life. Forgive me for rushing into work without first sitting with You.

I don't want to rely on my own strength when You've given me access to Yours. Show me how to prioritize You — not just when it's convenient, but when it's costly. Let my creativity flow from connection, not pressure.

I surrender my schedule, my plans, and my process. I want to abide in You and create from that place.

And as Your Word says: "Remain in me, as I also remain in you... If you remain in me and I in you, you will bear much fruit; apart from me you can do nothing." (John 15:4–5)

Keep me rooted in You, Lord, so that everything I create bears lasting fruit.

In Jesus' name, Amen.

CHAPTER 7:

RELEASE WHAT'S IN YOU — CREATING FROM LEGACY

"For God's gifts and his call can never be withdrawn."
(Romans 11:29, NLT)

There's a kind of weight that comes with carrying something God has placed in you.

It's beautiful, but it's also sobering. Because when God gives you something — a gift, an idea, a story, a calling — it's not just for you. It's a seed with the potential to bear fruit far beyond what your eyes can see.

That's what legacy is in the Kingdom.

Not fame. Not status. Not a name etched in lights. But a life poured out in obedience.

WHAT LEGACY REALLY MEANS

Let's be clear. When we talk about legacy here, we're not talking about building empires or being remembered by the masses. We're talking about obedient stewardship with eternity in mind.

Kingdom legacy is this:

- It's what your yes is building.

- It's the ripple effect of your obedience.

- It's the unseen seeds that God multiplies — in the earth and in eternity.

Legacy is the story God continues to write through your life, long after the moment of release has passed.

Legacy is raising children in prayer.
Legacy is creating from conviction.
Legacy is choosing faithfulness over applause.

And often, legacy grows in places you'll never see.

THE PARABLE OF THE TALENTS: WHAT DID YOU DO WITH WHAT GOD GAVE YOU?

In Matthew 25:14–30, Jesus tells the story of a master who entrusts three servants with talents — one receives five, one receives two, and one receives one. The first two invest and multiply what they've been given. But the last one? He buries his.

When the master returns, he praises the first two: "Well done, good and faithful servant."

But the third servant says something that always grabs me:
"I was afraid... so I hid it."

That line right there — that's where so many of us have lived.

- Afraid we're not good enough.

- Afraid it won't be received well.

- Afraid of failing.

- Afraid of succeeding and not knowing what to do next.

So we bury the very thing we were called to build.

And Jesus makes it plain: God is not pleased when we bury what He gave us, no matter how small it seems.

You weren't asked to be successful by the world's standards. You were asked to be faithful with what was entrusted to you.

FAITHFULNESS IS THE ASSIGNMENT

What if the poem, the podcast, the painting, the program, the business, the book… wasn't about what it does, but who it touches?

What if the fruit of your release isn't loud, but it's lasting?

Maybe no one applauded.
Maybe it didn't go viral.
Maybe it felt like it fell flat.

But if God told you to release it, then it wasn't wasted.

Because the goal isn't to impress, the goal is to multiply what He gave you. To move in obedience. To build a legacy.

There's someone on the other side of your release.
Someone who needs what's in you.
 Someone who's waiting for you to stop burying and
start building.

THIS IS THE TIME TO RELEASE

You've been sitting on it long enough.

That journal.
That idea.
That draft.
That story.
That song.

It doesn't have to be perfect.
It just has to be released.

You were never called to keep it to yourself.
You were called to carry it — and then pour it out.

You are not behind.
You are not invisible.
You are not empty.

You've just been holding back.

And now, it's time to release what's in you.

Not just for now.
Not just for you.
But for legacy.

REFLECTION QUESTIONS

- What have I been burying out of fear, and what would it look like to release it in faith?

- Have I been measuring my success by outcomes or by obedience?

- What seed am I being asked to plant today that could shape someone else's tomorrow?

LET'S PRAY

God, thank You for trusting me with what You've placed in my hands. I don't want to bury it out of fear. I want to be faithful. I want to build a legacy with you.

Remind me that legacy isn't about being known — it's about making You known. Help me release what You've given me, even if it feels small or imperfect. I surrender the fear, the pressure, and the hesitation. Teach me to steward my gift like a good and faithful servant.

And may it be said of me, "Well done, good and faithful servant. You have been faithful with a few things; I will put you in charge of many things. Come and share your Master's happiness." (Matthew 25:21)

I choose obedience over outcome. Faithfulness over fear. Legacy over performance.

CONCLUSION:

A FINAL CHARGE

"For we are God's masterpiece. He has created us anew in Christ Jesus, so we can do the good things He planned for us long ago." (Ephesians 2:10, NLT)

You were never just meant to watch other people create. You weren't created to play small, shrink back, or bury what God placed inside of you. You were created to create.

This book hasn't been about perfection or performance. It's been about reminding you of your identity — the creative imprint of a God who made you in His image. From the beginning, creativity was part of your design. It's not extra. It's embedded. And what's embedded is meant to be multiplied.

Jesus tells a sobering story in Matthew 25 — the Parable of the Talents. A master entrusted his servants with different amounts of money before going away. Two of them invested what they were given and multiplied it. One of them hid what he had out of fear and insecurity.

And when the master returned, he asked for an account.

He wanted to know: What did you do with what I gave you?

That question still echoes today.

God has placed something in you — something real, something needed, something that carries solutions for this generation. And he didn't give it to you for safekeeping. He gave it to you to multiply it. To move with it. To release it into the earth.

Your gift is not random.
Your creativity is not optional.
Your obedience is not invisible.

It all matters. And there will come a time when we stand before the Master and He'll ask what we did with what He gave us.

Not to shame us.
But because He believed in us.
Because he invested in us.

You were never creating just for now. You're creating for legacy. You're building what will outlast you. You're planting seeds that will grow into fruit someone else will eat.

This is your charge:
Create anyway.
Move anyway.
Obey anyway.

Even when you don't feel ready.
Even when the outcome looks different from what you hoped.
Even when no one claps, no one comments, and it feels like no one sees.

Because Heaven is watching.
And Heaven is waiting for your yes.

FITTLY JOINED TOGETHER

And remember this: you are not creating in isolation.

Paul reminds us in Ephesians 4:16 that we are "fitly joined together, and compacted by that which every joint supplieth… making increase of the body unto the edifying of itself in love."

That means there is no competition in the Kingdom. Each of us has a particular role to play — a unique gift to steward — but together we make up one body.

Your creativity doesn't diminish anyone else's; it strengthens the whole. Their obedience doesn't overshadow yours; it complements it.

When you release what God placed in you, you don't just build your legacy — you equip the body. And together, we point back to the One who created us all.

So release your gift boldly, knowing it's not just about you. It's about us. The body. The Kingdom. The generations to come.

FINAL DECLARATION

I was created to create. I am a vessel of God's creativity, chosen for this moment. I will no longer hide what He has entrusted to me. I will multiply the gift, release the vision, and obey the call — because Heaven is waiting on my yes. I am not creating for applause. I'm creating for legacy. And I will be found faithful.

ACTIVATION PRAYER

Father, thank You for trusting me with this gift. Forgive me for the times I buried it out of fear, shame, doubt, or distraction. I don't want to waste what you've invested in me. I want to be found faithful, like the servants who multiplied what was entrusted to their care (Matthew 25:14–30).

Teach me to use my gift as 1 Peter 4:10 says — faithfully administering Your grace in its various forms. Remind me that You chose me and appointed me to bear fruit, fruit that will last (John 15:16).

I commit to multiply what You've entrusted, not for applause but for impact. Let my creativity become an offering — not just of talent, but of trust. Not just of beauty, but of faith.

May everything I create point back to You. May the fruit of my obedience strengthen the body of Christ, impact generations, and glorify Your name. And when I stand before You, I long to hear, "Well done, good and faithful servant."

In Jesus' name, Amen.

www.ingramcontent.com/pod-product-compliance
Lightning Source LLC
Chambersburg PA
CBHW071534120626
46550CB00006B/2458